PRINCE EDWARD ISLAND
Red Soil, Blue Sea, Green Fields.

Prince Edward Island

Red Soil, Blue Sea, Green Fields.

Photographs by
Wayne Barrett and Anne MacKay

Foreword by David Weale

Nimbus Publishing Limited
Halifax

South Melville

RIGHT:
Queen Anne's Lace

Nimbus Publishing Limited
P.O. Box 9301, Stn. A
Halifax, Nova Scotia
Canada B3K5N5

Canadian Cataloguing in Publication Data

Barrett, Wayne
    Prince Edward Island
    ISBN 0-921054-05-X

1. Prince Edward Island—Description and
Travel—1981—Views.* I. MacKay, Anne.
II. Title
FC2612.B37 1988   971.7:04:0222
C88-098549-6   F1047.8.B37 1988

Design: Design Associates Limited

Printing and Binding: Everbest Printing
Company Limited, Hong Kong

PRECEDING PAGES:
Park Corner

To Jason and Amy with love

ACKNOWLEDGEMENTS

We wish to thank the following people and organizations who assisted in the preparation of this book: Confederation Centre of the Arts; Prince Edward Island Department of Tourism and Parks; Dorothy Cooper, our Publisher; Tonya Mutch and Shelley Campbell, for their valued input; Don Smith for his design and Takaharu Yamaguchi for the hours he devoted to the artwork. We also thank our families and children for their love and encouragement.

Photography in this book has been reproduced from 35mm and 6 × 7cm Kodachrome and Fujichrome transparencies.

Listen to the Island
And you may hear
The music of creation
Hanging in the air on gulls' wings.

Gull

Song of the Island by David Weale

Look at the Island
Soft red stone
You can break with your fingers
Derelict dunes
Shuffling in the wind
And fields
Thin-carpeted
Running down to the sculpturing sea.

Look carefully and you will see
This is not a hard place.

The carved shoreline tells the story.
There is no granite resistance
To wind and water
No invincible stand against the elements.
Just a dignified falling back
Into coves and bays
And the dull booming of the tide
In ten thousand scoured caves
Beneath ten thousand wafered ledges.

It was God created Abegweit
Raised it up all shimmering and wet
Like a mirage.

But it was Islanders
Made the Island
Made it over to suit themselves.

There is no place more plowed and pruned
No place more touched
It has all been combed and curried
And braided like a mane.

It is everywhere visible
The signature of sweat and dreams
Written like a road
Up and down
From one end to the other.

They are quilters
These Islanders
Stretching out the landscape
In the maple frame of intention

Squaring it off in fields and wood-lots
And stitching all around with perseverance.

And when they look at what they have done together
View it at a glance
From the brow of a hill
Or from the sky
There is surprise and wonder
At the perfection
Of the larger design.

In the beginning
They hurled themselves at the forest
Waging war with fire and steel
Driving back the trees with a shout.
Then they trampled and tractored it flat
And there are old bruises not healed
And fresh blade wounds
Bleeding far out into the Strait.

But this low furrowed land
Gentle and vulnerable
Begets the caring heart
And a spirit
Which grieves for harms caused
Those who cannot feel it
Are strangers here
Though their forebears stepped ashore
Two hundred years ago.

Small infinite place
There is no end to the wonder you evoke
Or the ways you point
Beyond yourself
To that eternal light
Which shines like silver on the tidal flats
And brushes the dunes all pink
In evening softness.

Small human place
Of watchers in windows
And conversation which rolls down slowly
Like potatoes on a pile.
There is no wilderness here

Just walking down lanes
To mailboxes
And neighbours waving from the car.

Small stormy place
With mares' tails flying
And wet blowy days
After a wet moon.
And when the March wind sweeps across the fields
And the snow streams low like a tide
There is a ritual of grumbling
To pass away the sentence of winter detention.

Small coloured place
Where eager green
Spreads out like ferns unfurled
And flowers
All wild and bare-headed
Like children on vacation
Are scattered in joy and laud
During holy days of goldenrod.

Small summer place
The sea unlocked
And waves sliding up to children's feet.
There are two worlds here
A festival of play, and one of work
Of tents and trailers and tickets to Anne
And half-ton trucks
On the wharf at ten to four.

Small enchanted place
You rise in the moon to ancient music
And dance the dance
Of the generations
Elbow in elbow
Swinging back through time
To the place
Where first you heard the song.

Listen to the Island
And you may hear
The music of creation
Hanging in the air on gulls' wings.

FOLLOWING PAGES:
Meadowbank

9

East Point Light

The carved shoreline tells the story.
There is no granite resistance
To wind and water
No invincible stand against the elements
Just a dignified falling back
Into coves and bays.

Brudenell

Riverdale

Then they trampled and tractored it flat
And there are old bruises not healed
And fresh blade wounds
Bleeding far out into the Strait.

LEFT:
Kildare Capes

Norboro

The signature of sweat and dreams
Written like a road
Up and down
From one end to the other.

New Glasgow

Look carefully and you will see
This is not a hard place.

Churchill

FOLLOWING PAGES:
South Melville

West River, Dunedin

West River

Small infinite place
There is no end to the wonder you evoke.

St. Peters Bay

. . .that eternal light
which shines like silver on the tidal flats.

North Rustico

Dalvay pond

Strathgartney

New Glasgow

And when the cold March wind sweeps across the fields
And the snow streams low like a tide
There is a ritual of grumbling
To pass away the sentence of winter detention.

New Haven

Miscouche

Hope River

Cavendish, Prince Edward Island National Park

And the dull booming of the tide
In ten thousand scoured caves
Beneath ten thousand wafered ledges.

Guernsey Cove

There is no place more plowed and pruned
No place more touched
It has all been combed and curried
And braided like a mane.

near Crapaud

They are quilters
These Islanders
Stretching out the landscape
In the maple frame of intention
Squaring it off in fields and wood-lots
And stitching all around with perseverance.

LEFT:
Harry Fraser, potato farmer

North Lake

Small human place
Of watchers in windows
And conversation which rolls down slowly
Like potatoes on a pile.

LEFT:
Cherry Valley

Wood Islands

Field of Lupines, Granville

RIGHT:
Lady's Slipper orchid

Orwell

And flowers
All wild and bare-headed
Like children on vacation
Are scattered in joy and laud

Fern

Small coloured place
Where eager green
Spreads out like ferns unfurled.

RIGHT:
Wildflowers

Wild rose

Cedar Waxwing in apple tree

Mergansers and Goldeneye ducks

Dolphins, North Lake

FOLLOWING PAGES:
Harp seal and pup

Harvesting Irish Moss, Miminegash

New Haven

Dog team races, Charlottetown Winter Carnival

Ice boat races, Charlottetown Harbour

Confederation Plaza, Charlottetown

Small enchanted place
You rise in the moon to ancient music
And dance the dance
Of the generations.

LEFT:
Canadian Heritage Festival, Acadian Pioneer Village, Mont-Carmel

The Play, "Anne of Green Gables,"
Confederation Centre of the Arts

LEFT:
Scottish dancer, Lord Selkirk Provincial Park

FOLLOWING PAGES:
Charlottetown

Corner of Grafton and Queen, Charlottetown

There are two worlds here
A festival of play, and one of work.

Hon. George Coles Building, Charlottetown

Confederation Centre of the Arts, Charlottetown

RIGHT:
Confederation Centre Art Gallery

Joyce Wieland

Province House, Charlottetown

But it was Islanders
Made the Island
Made it over to suit themselves.

Confederation Centre of the Arts

Vera Stephenson as "Tammy"
in the play, "Babies,"
Confederation Centre of the Arts

Charlottetown

All Soul's Chapel, St. Peter's Cathedral,
Charlottetown

Victoria

It was God created Abegweit
Raised it up all shimmering and wet
Like a mirage.

Beaconsfield, Charlottetown

Government House, Charlottetown

Summerside

Presbyterian Church, Clyde River

Stanhope

Charlottetown

Panmure Island

LEFT:
St. Patrick's Roman Catholic Church, Grand River

Freetown

In the beginning
They hurled themselves at the wilderness
Waging war with fire and steel.
Driving back the trees with a shout.

LEFT:
Long River

West Royalty

Wheatley River

And when they look at what they have done together
View it at a glance
From the brow of a hill
Or from the sky
There is a surprise and wonder
At the perfection
Of the larger design.

LEFT:
Marshfield

Brookfield

LEFT:
Race horse, Charlottetown Driving Park

Charlottetown Driving Park, Old Home Week

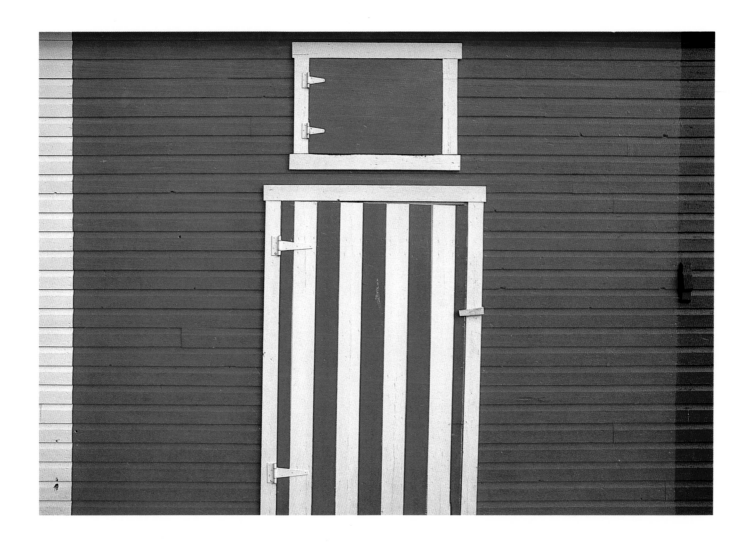

Beach Point

Beach Point

Rural Mail Box

There is no wilderness here
Just walking down lanes
To mailboxes
And neighbours waving from the car.

LEFT:
Weather vane

Montague

Rainbow trout

LEFT:
North Lake

Carousel horses, country fair

Horseback riding, St. Catherines

Glen Valley

Cousin's Shore, Park Corner

Small summer place
The sea unlocked
And waves sliding up to children's feet.

"Setting day", North Rustico

FOLLOWING PAGES:
Tracadie

North Shore dunes

Derelict dunes
Shuffling in the wind

Sand Spit, Cavendish

Bow of a fishing boat, Morel

LEFT:
West Point Lighthouse Festival Boat Races

Water filled dory, West River

Murray Harbour

And half-ton trucks
On the wharf at ten to four.

Tuna fishing, North Lake

LEFT:
Tuna reel

Tuna fishing, North Lake

LEFT:
Captain Harvey Pool, North Lake

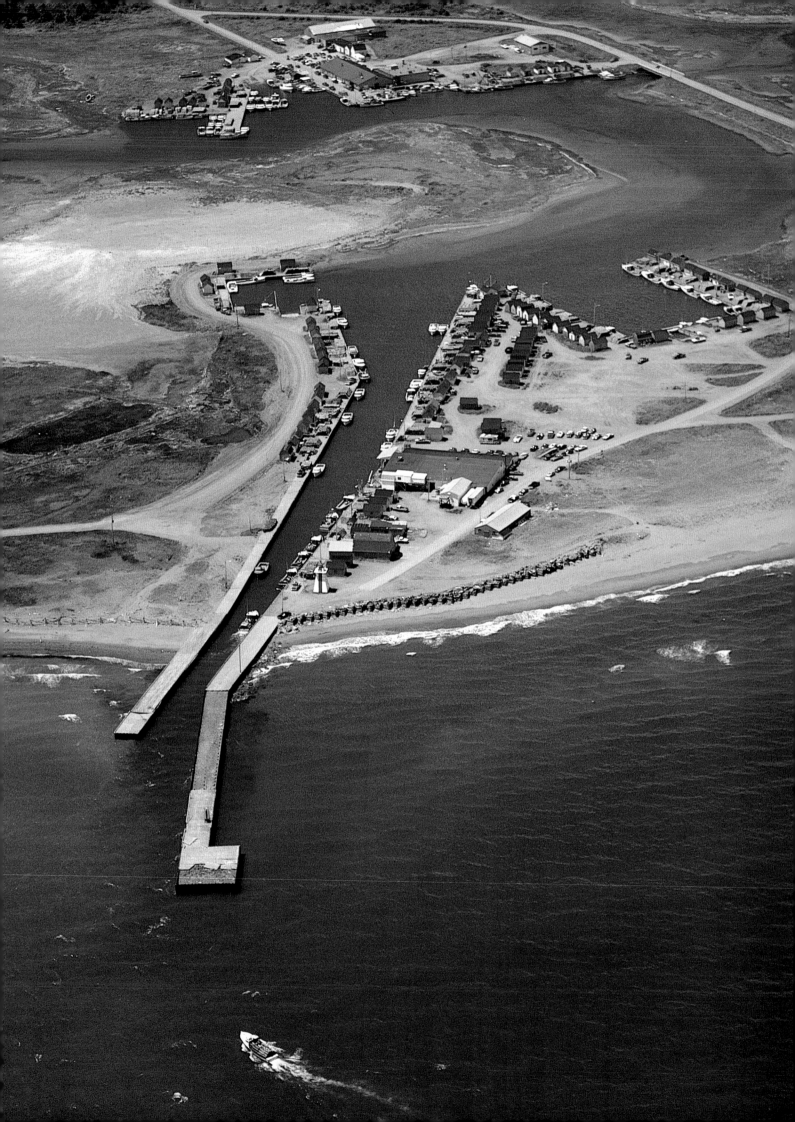

The ferry, *Lucy Maude Montgomery,* leaving Souris

LEFT:
Tignish Run

Summerside

Point Prim Light

Soft red stone
You can break with your fingers

Cape Egmont

But this low furrowed land
Gentle and vulnerable
Begets the caring heart.